YOU JUST MIGHT BE A DEMOCRAT

ISBN: 978-1-7331452-9-9

Including ***My Daddy Always Said*** *Satire*

Dedication/Introduction

WARNING

STAY BACK TWO HUNDRED MILES
NOT RESPONSIBLE FOR

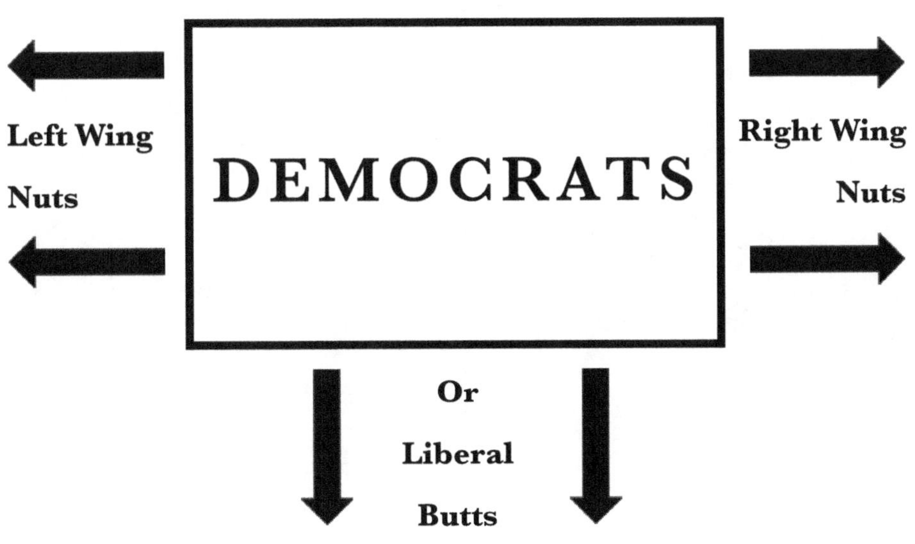

If you have to spread your ass cheeks in order to scratch your head, you just might be a Democrat.

My daddy always said when Mitch McConnell sent Nancy Pelosi a note asking her to send over a no brainer bill ASAP, Nancy said, "Mitch, I don't have a no brainer Bill working for me. Will a no brainer A.O.C. work for you?

If you are Speaker of the House and you stepped on your tail, fell down, broke one of your horns, and nobody noticed, you just might be a Democrat.

My daddy always said if you are the high cheek bone Native American fake-a-hontas Warren, out helping the Chief gather maize for the first Thanksgiving feast and you bent over to get your bung hole tanned before dinner, would the Chief say to you, "Fake-e-baby, your maize hole is puckered," or would he say, "wild and crazy woman, your corn hole is puckered?"

If you see a car on the side of the road with a sign in the rear window that reads "out of gas please help," and you stop and give them a can of beans, you just might be a Democrat.

If your hemorrhoids were a gift from constipation and you can't find anyone to regift them to, you just might be a Democrat.

My daddy always said if you are a Democrat, do your part… practice social distancing before you fart.

If you are like Nancy Pelosi and everything you eat turns to Schiff, you just might be a Democrat.

If you entered a bean bag contest and found out that the bean bags riot police use travel faster than you can run, you just might be a Democrat.

If you have spent your entire life trying to convince people "that you weren't born last night," you just might be a Democrat.

My daddy always said he would have been in shock if he had known how to spell it, when his boss told him to go home and self-quarantine with soap and water for the rest of his life.

If you put your wig in the dishwasher and all you got back was a mustache, you just might be a Democrat.

If your Santa Claus used six rats and a red nose rodent to pull his sled to your house, you just might be a Democrat.

If Babs and Cher fanned you while you were getting your bunghole suntanned, you just might be a Democrat.

My daddy always said when Katie Hill was on Capitol Hill, was she working on a Bill or working on a beaver?

If you are not Sharon Stone and your basic ass stinks, you just might be a Democrat.

If your daddy named you Worthless because he wanted you to be a carbon copy of him, you just might be a Democrat.

If your garden knowledge doesn't go beyond the dumb ass in your Fruit of the Loom underwear, you just might be a Democrat.

If you are one of the people that use Bengay for hemorrhoid ointment, you just might be a Democrat.

If you spent the weekend in a "weak end," you just might be a Democrat.

My daddy always said what are grandparents saying about babies being born to their millennial children? Joy to the world! How many years do we have to wait to know if it's a boy or girl?

If you became an anal-yst because you are obsessed with sticking your nose in the first four letters, you just might be a Democrat.

If the wind beneath your wings is from the fart above your knees, you just might be a Democrat.

If the Walmart greeter gave you a bar of soap with picture directions on how to take a bath, you just might be a Democrat.

If you're at the all you can eat buffet and rattle the windows with a fart because you want to thin the line, you just might be a Democrat.

If your sanctuary city is located between your ass cheeks, you just might be a Democrat.

If you were born holding the short end of the stick and you believe one of your ears is smarter than the other, you just might be a Democrat.

If your momma's nickname at the White House Oval Office was deepthroat, you just might be a Democrat.

If your ratchet is wore-out from trying to keep all those loose screw balls tight in Washington D.C. until the election is over, you just might be a Democrat.

My daddy always said the only thing you have to fear is the credit card bill at the end of the month and the sight of Nancy Pelosi's face before you have time to get drunk.

If Ted Turner won't die so Jane Fonda can fake a cry and Nancy won't yield the gavel so Schiff can get a feel for power and you believe Democrats never lie, you just might be a Democrat.

If you are at your local Department of Motor Vehicles and you think the line is moving too fast, you just might be a Democrat.

If you think Mount Rush-more means having sex with a horse, you just might be a Democrat.

My daddy always said what do the bathroom scales say when Hillary steps on to weigh herself? "Please, one at a time."

If you are sitting in your car and you see a display on your dash that reads 'door ajar' and you have smoked enough mo-crat to believe your door is a "jar," you just might be a D-mo-crat.

If the bird in your hand is a buzzard and the two in your bush are Billy and slick Willie, and you don't have a clue how they got there, you just might be a Democrat.

If you are having trouble learning a new language, you should try bunghole speaking. Bunghole speaking will help you talk like a Democrat – walk like a Democrat – lie like a Democrat and in no time at all you will be fluent. Here's how to order: 1-800- you just might be a Democrat.

My daddy always said what did the hooker say to the judge when she was charged with selling her ass as a high fiber $500.00 thirty-minute diet? "Your honor, good fiber don't come cheap."

If you go hunting in yoga pants and high heels, you just might be a Democrat.

If your mother gave birth to your wife and you are from New York, you just might be a Democrat.

If you are Martha Stewart and your dog won't Snoop, Katie won't brush your hair, Hillary won't sit, bark, or beg, and Chris with his coffee cup won't crawl up your leg, you just might be a Democrat.

If you are from the hood and your better half is from the trunk and your kids are from the back seat, you just might be a Democrat.

My daddy always said if you pick your nose on Halloween does that make you a booger man?

My daddy always said that a difference that makes no difference is no difference at all, unless you are a politician needing money.

If you are Nanny P, and you walk around quoting 'to pee or not to pee,' to Schiff or not to Schiff,' 'to A.O.C. or not to A.O.C.,' and you think people don't know that's a dead beaver on your head… Nanny, you just might be a Democrat.

If you are using one regular square of toilet tissue to wipe your Time Square size ass, you just might be a Democrat.

If you believe the interstate was built just for you to drive in the left lane at any speed you desire, you just might be a Democrat.

If your New York cousin got knocked up in the parking lot of an In-and-Out convenient store by her Uncle Joe from Delaware, you just might be a Democrat.

If you are feeling sick because you have been watching, listening, and believing the words that come from the piles of Schiff in Congress, you just might be a Democrat.

My daddy always said old crazy Joe Biden recently gave advice on how to get your stimulus check faster. "Get yourself a double barrel shotgun. Shove it up your ass. Fire off two blasts- one to the left, one to the right, and see which one sends you a Coronavirus check first."

If you fight a brush fire by pissing in the wind, you just might be a Democrat.

My daddy always said what does a Democrat politician say to his voters at election time? Remember fools, when nothing goes right in your life keep going left.

If you are a farmer's daughter and you like sex so much you can't keep your calves together, you just might be a Democrat.

If your hell hole is located below your nose, you just might be a Democrat.

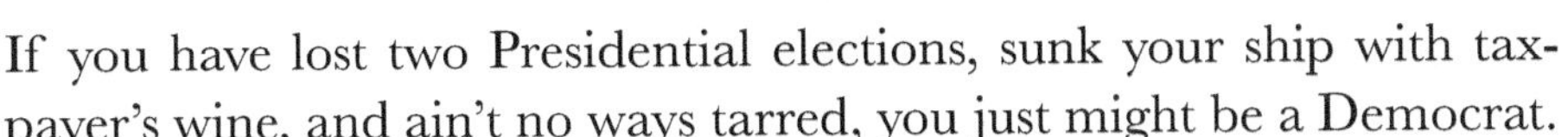

If you have lost two Presidential elections, sunk your ship with taxpayer's wine, and ain't no ways tarred, you just might be a Democrat.

If the road you live on is a dead end and the only hair that gets parted is on your head and everything you eat turns to Schiff, and A.O.C. won't bark for you like Hillary did, you just might be a Democrat.

If you shake your moneymaker down at the strip club and all you make is noise, you just might be a Democrat.

My daddy always said President Clinton proved at least one thing with Monica Lewinsky. Americans will do the Oval Office oral jobs that all those illegal aliens just won't do.

If you believe all the lies the Democrats tell are for your ears only, you just might be a Democrat.

If you are so dumb that the only half of a word you know is mother, you just might be a Democrat.

If you are the reporter that tried to contact the dead for a comment, you just might be a Democrat.

If you are married to your sister's mother, you just might be a Democrat.

My daddy always said while Katie Hill was mowing hair, weaker of the House, Nanny P., was cleaning up piles of Schiff while burping the squad. That's when she discovered that all her 'homies' were just like old ball-less Ford. They all graduated from di-fi-lying Stein's school of don't ever tell the truth.

If your family tree is a ragweed, you just might be a Democrat.

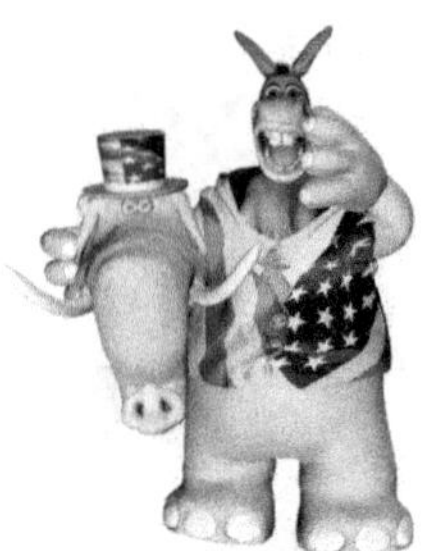

If everybody but you calls your darling, darling, you just might be a Democrat.

My daddy always said that he has used so much hand sanitizer that now every time he farts it smells like Purell.

If your mama got drunk the day you were born to celebrate the day she was drunk when she got pregnant, you just might be a Democrat.

If your name is Robert O'Rourke and you never learned how to spell or pronounce it, you just might be a Democrat.

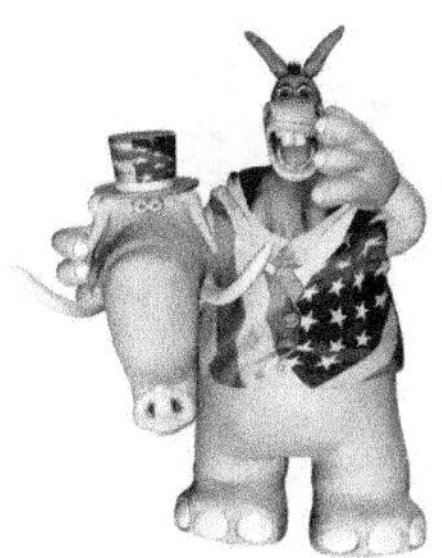

If your head has been pulled from Nancy Pelosi's ass so many times that you have developed a pencil neck, you just might be a Democrat.

If you treat your elected office as a key to the taxpayer's funds for your personal wants, needs, and desires, you just might be a Democrat.

If the entire Chinese buffet is smaller than your ass, you just might be a Democrat.

If your life's ambition is to train snails to arm wrestle, you just might be a Democrat.

If your neighbor is your pimp, your parole officer, your daddy, and your landlord, you just might be Democrat.

If your summer job is collecting unemployment checks, you just might be a Democrat.

If you climb a tree in order to tell a lie when you could have stayed on the ground and told the truth, you just might be a Democrat.

My daddy always said this morning I got up at 6:02, couldn't think of a thing to do so I began to beat my old dog. It wasn't long before she was pissed and took the stick and left me with the Joe Biden look. Now I'm needing hair plugs where she took the hair off my ass. The moral of the story: don't ever beat your wife if you value your life.

If the only Native American you know is fake-a-hontas Warren, you just might be a Democrat.

If a snail crawls faster than your brain works, you just might be a Democrat.

If the odor under your arms will gag a maggot, you just might be a Democrat.

My daddy always said the boss makes a dollar; I make a dime. That's why I can't afford to buy any wine, women or song. Now you all know why my ding won't dong, because I don't have the wine – the women or the song.

If there are too many lips kissing your ass while you're speaking to the House, you just might be a Democrat.

If your heroes have always been Democrats, you just might be a Democrat.

If you pick grandma's nose to entertain the left side of your brain, you just might be a Democrat.

If you don't know how to operate the turn signals on the car you drive, you just might be a Democrat.

If you can't read the sign on the back of a truck that says, "Caution: Wide Right Turn," you just might be a Democrat.

My daddy always said if a he is considered a dictator then what is a she considered, a putator?

If the Schiff you stepped in belongs to Nancy Pelosi and you didn't Quid-pro-quo it before you flew off to Ukraine, you just might be a Democrat.

If it's your duty to clean your booty and you only half-ass it, you just might be a Democrat.

My daddy always said when a Democrat donkey is smelling another donkey's ass, what are they sniffing for; mo-money or some honey?

If you think stop signs and red lights are for everybody but you, you just might be a Democrat.

If you are smiling when the doctor is performing a prostate exam, you just might be a Democrat.

If you point your finger at the TV camera and say to America that you didn't have sex with that woman, you just might be a Democrat.

If you don't know the difference between common sense, good sense or 50 Cent, you just might be a Democrat.

If the fork in the road has better eating manners than you, you just might be a Democrat.

If the turkey you had for Thanksgiving was roadkill that Harvey Weinstein's walker ran over, you just might be a Democrat.

If the police placed a warning sticker on your car that reads, "Warning: Democrat Driving," you just might be a Democrat.

My daddy always said I've had a large mouth bass want to kiss my ass but due to the smell of my tail, the Democrats beat him to it.

If you stepped in a pile of shifting Schiff, and it's not sand, you just might be a Democrat.

If you see dollar signs when you read a warning label on a product, you just might be a Democrat.

If the wind coming from either set of your cheeks smells like dead fish, you just might be a Democrat.

If your momma wore a jockstrap on her honeymoon, you just might be a Democrat.

If you identified as Native American to receive free college tuition, then you identified as white to get elected to the Senate, and then you identified as honest to run for President, you just might be a Democrat.

My daddy always said what did Katie Hill learn from her short time in Congress? Be careful of who, when, and where you eat.

If the giant tree you fell out of was the 'tree of life,' and after falling, you realized it had been fertilized by fake Lizzy's lies, you just might be a Democrat.

If your Stacy size ass is used to measure the size of the National debt, you just might be a Democrat.

My daddy always said what did shifter Schiff say to life alert when he fell from grace? "Help! I lied and I can't stop lying, lying, and lying."

If you lick the restroom janitor's fingers after they have eaten fried chicken, you just might be a Democrat.

If she said in the Oval Office, I'll huff and I'll puff until I blow your balls off… you guessed it, she just might be a Democrat.

If you believe renewable energy is a Big Mac with fries, or hot wings and apple pies, you just might be a Democrat.

If you think being a Conservative means turning off the light, you just might be a Democrat.

If your only goal in life is to get drunk and stay high, you just might be a Democrat.

If counting the ways you hate Trump is at the top of your list, you just might be a Democrat.

If your girlfriend says - if you love me, let me ho – if you don't, let me run for Congress, you just might be a Democrat.

If you find no love at the ballot box and there is nothing as cold as their asses after the Democrats have gone back to their offices, you just might be a Democrat.

If you can't tell the truth, even when you're asleep, you just might be a Democrat.

If your monkey's uncle is your brother, you just might be a Democrat.

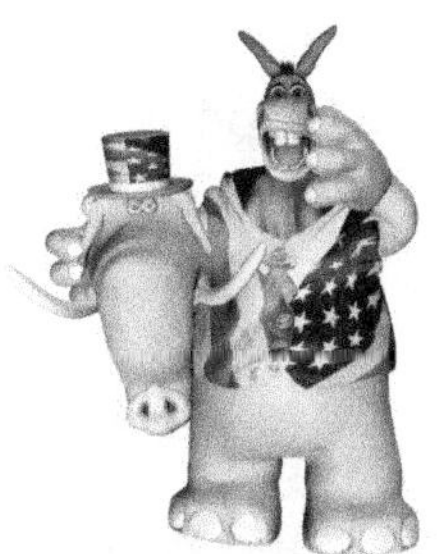

My daddy always said the Democrats have found and stopped their leaks. After extensive investigation, they found it was only Schiff putting in the wrong size tampon.

If you are a shifty Schiff and you serve under Nancy – (Queeeen of pull my finger) and no amount of soap can wash away that smell, you just might be a Democrat.

My daddy always said that doctor's test results show that 98% of Democrats in Congress tested positive for the stupid virus. The other two percent couldn't R. or R. their names or the questions on the test.

If the baby turds you use for your poop on Texas toast came from the kitchen of Beto, you just might be a Democrat.

If shifty, a.k.a. pencil neck, a.k.a. liar – liar pants on fire, stands before the TV cameras, points his finger and says, "I didn't satire Nancy Pelosi's ass," and you believe him, you just might be a Democrat.

If every time you open your mouth you end up getting stitches, you just might be a Democrat.

If you are plagued with lead-ass disease, you just might be a Democrat.

If you won't submit to the black light nose challenge, to check for brown matter, you just might be a 'pencil neck' Democrat.

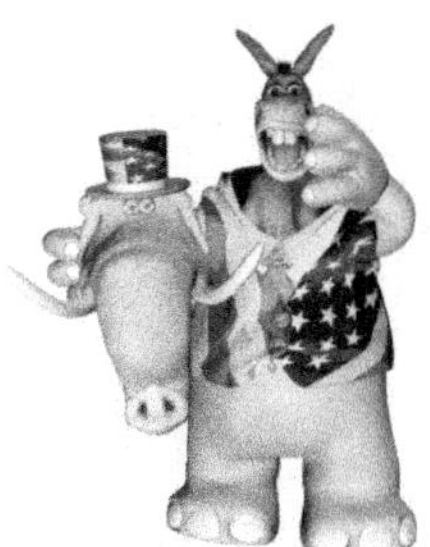

If you wait to buy your false teeth from a funeral home in order to save some money from your gov – ment check, you just might be a Democrat.

If you believe donating your skid marked underwear to Goodwill is an honest tax deduction, you just might be a Democrat.

If you have to use an air-pump to inflate your wife before sex, you just might be a Democrat.

My daddy always said when walking in the halls of Congress, watch where you step. There are piles of Schiff everywhere, and no matter what was used to clean his shoes, he never got the stench out.

If you are Chuck-U-Schumer and Nancy Pelosi is your highway and you ride her every night just so you won't lose your place in traffic, you just might be a Democrat.

If you can't get past the understanding of "it," you just might be a Democrat.

If you think your mole is bigger than your mountain, you just might be a Democrat.

My daddy always said some Democrats can't tell the difference between turds and words or 'which end' 'which one' comes from.

If your ass is big enough to have its own zip code, you just might be a Democrat.

If the only stock you own is the kind you make soup with, you just might be a Democrat.

If you believe anything or everything a Democrat says, you just might be a Democrat.

If you don't know the difference between Santa Claus and a sanity clause, you just might be a Democrat.

If you walk the halls of Congress with the words 'easy loving' on your lapel, you just might be a Democrat.

If your momma used you for a doorstop when you were a baby, you just might be a Democrat.

If you think your daddy bought you the Brooklyn Bridge and you're trying to sell it on eBay, you just might be a Democrat.

If it's your duty to put your lips on Nancy Pelosi's booty, you just might be a Democrat.

My daddy always said when a new business opened in town, they put signs on their fence that said, "We operate on the honor system. If you honor this fence, we will honor your life."

If you know a lie is a lie and you swear it's the truth, you just might be a Democrat.

My daddy always said when a reporter asked a newly elected Democrat member of Congress what they had to offer the American people, their answer was, "I have this and that to offer to the American people." The reporter asked, "What is your this and what is your that?" To which the congress member answered, "Well, this ain't that and that ain't this." The reporter replied, "Ms. A.O.C., you will make a great Democrat Congresswoman."

If you were standing behind Nanny-pee-loosely when she blew her Frog-horn and you said it was only lard ball's coffee cup, not a fart, you just might be a Democrat.

If you believe Rosie O'Donnell got her fish breath from eating sardines, you just might be a Democrat.

If you think the truth is something you throw under the bus, and a lie is something you wear like a badge of honor, you just might be a Democrat.

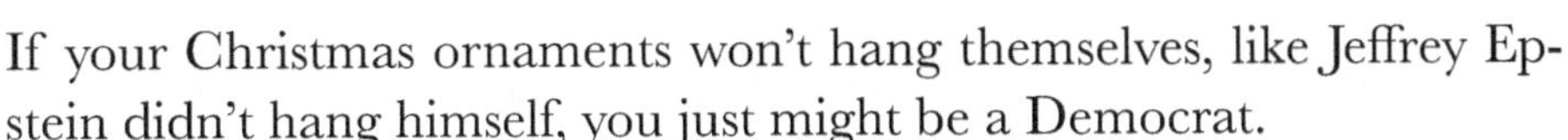

If your Christmas ornaments won't hang themselves, like Jeffrey Epstein didn't hang himself, you just might be a Democrat.

If only half your ass is behind your back, you just might be a Democrat.

If the food you sit down to eat is prepared by the 'agony' of them on their feet, you just might be a Democrat.

If the holes in your underwear are from a K-9 biting your ass because it was chasing you down, trying to get the bank's money back, you just might be a Democrat.

My daddy always said when Felicity Hoffman farted in the Federal Correction Institution and none of the alpha bets of the teleprompter readers were there to smell it, heads rolled. Some wound up on the floor – some out the door, but all of them asked to be imbedded in her prison uniform so they would be the first to get her tail smell.

If you believe that the world is full of assholes and idiots and you are merely the conductor of them, you just might be a Democrat.

If the air you breathe comes from just above Nancy Pelosi's knees, you just might be a Democrat.

If you get your message from a booty, instead of a bottle, you just might be a Democrat.

If you believe Hillary doesn't have wine jowls and Pete doesn't judge butts, you just might be a Democrat.

If you bought underwear at a yard sell and those skid marks aren't your skid marks, you just might be a Democrat.

If you believe the celebrities traveling in private jets and limousines are working on your behalf to help reverse climate change, you just might be a Democrat.

My daddy always said when President Trump declared a state of Nancy emergency to clean up all the Schiff that she let collect on her caboose – Chuck-U-Schumer said that's not enough. The President should appoint old Debbie wash-a-woman Schultz to wash all that Schiff off Nanny's caboose.

If the hair on your ass is longer than the hair on your head, you just might be a Democrat.

If the teeth you use to chew your food belong to your grandma, you just might be a Democrat.

If you believe forever is a virgin and didn't give birth to yesterday, you just might be a Democrat.

My daddy always said they may be dead, buried in the ground, but they are still living rent free in D.C. town.

If you believe the government is a money tree and you are entitled to a bag full anytime you want it, you just might be a Democrat.

If the thong you're wearing is the same one your grandma wears when she's pole dancing, you just might be a Democrat.

If you woke up with bed bugs in your hair, you've been somewhere you shouldn't have been or, you just might be a Democrat.

If you can't walk down the street in San Francisco, California without stepping in a pile of Schiff and you keep voting that Schiff into office, you just might be a Democrat.

If would - could, should it? If could - should, would it? If should - would, could it? If you can't solve the riddle, of 'M' in your peach as the first half of the first word you learned to pronounce when you were elected to Congress, you just might be a Democrat.

If you are from New York and you write your empty wine bottles off on your taxes with the names of float-my-boat and screw-u-all, you just might be a Democrat.

My daddy always said Harvey Weinstein has donated his walker to Prince Andrew and Slick Willie – since the walker got him 23, he is hoping it will do the same for his brothers from another mother.

If you get constipated every time you hear the truth, you just might be a Democrat.

If your better half is your left hand, you just might be a Democrat.

If you can't get past the – A - to "B" somebody, you just might be a Democrat.

If you are getting your loving from the south end of a northbound donkey, you just might be a Democrat.

My daddy always said listen to Pelosi on-living-in-tick-land. "Let me be clear. I've had so many face lifts that now my cooter sits on top of my head. The doctor said one more face lift and my cooter would be back where it started. When that happens, my nose won't be the escape hatch for what my ass farted.

If flies are following you everywhere you go, you could be a politician or, you just might be a Democrat.

If you and grandma are in the witness and wetness program - you the wetness, grandma the witness, you just might be a Democrat.

If you are the king of your castle, queen of your commode or the doofus that didn't flush the heavy load, you just might be a Democrat.

My daddy always said the only reason Elon Musk is taking Adam Schiff, Maxine Waters, and Nancy -pee- loosely on his maiden voyage to Mars is he needs pee and water for seeds to sprout and Schiff for fertilizer.

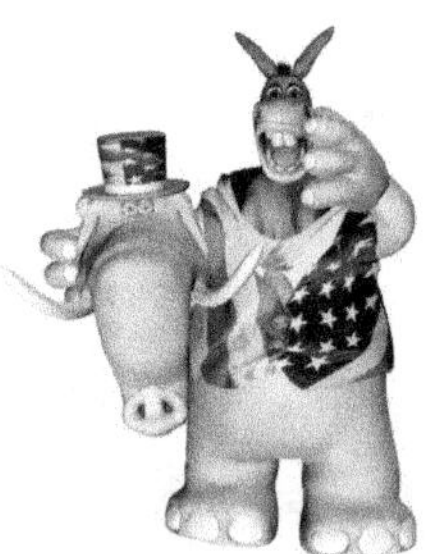

If you believe human rights is the opposite of no left turns, you just might be a Democrat.

If you brought your maid on your honeymoon because she makes you feel like a natural woman, you just might be a Democrat.

If all you have is a used Ford who lied to the whole world, you just might be a Democrat.

If you supported Hillary's inconvenient sized ass during her biggest loser campaign, you just might be a Democrat.

If you don't know what hole you're on, or what hole you're in, or what hole you've been in, or if the game is even over, you just might be a Democrat.

If you are a member of the D.E.D. - 'Don't Ever Do,' and you did your doo-doo in the po-po parking lot with the cameras watching, you just might be a Democrat.

My daddy always said why did the po-po arrest Santa Claus? For delivering the ho-ho-ho's that the Democrats in Congress ordered for Christmas.

If you use the hair under your arms for dental floss, you just might be a Democrat.

If the beaver you chased all night turned out to be a Pitbull at daybreak, you just might be a Democrat.

If you only see the side of the coin you believe to be the truth, you just might be a Democrat.

If you have to pay late charges on the false teeth you rented from the funeral home for your wedding, you just might be a Democrat.

If the waiter brought a plate of beans and you were rattling the glass in the windows before you left the restaurant, you just might be a Democrat.

My daddy always said – Warning: This product is for people with common sense; sorry Democrats.

If you gave your charitable donations to your favorite Charity, who happens to be a pole dancer down at the strip club, you just might be a Democrat.

If you have a two-hundred-pound warthog on your ass, it doesn't mean its Hillary, it simply means, you just might be a Democrat.

If you believe the world should be gluten-free but Russia should never be Putin free, you just might be a Democrat.

If the size of your ass is complementary of your neighborhood fast-food drive-thru, you just might be a Democrat.

If the ass in your turf has been worn down to the, 'I Can't Believe It's Nut Butter,' and nobody wants to play ball on your turf anymore, you just might be a Democrat.

If you're Nancy Pelosi and after the doctor saw your x-rays he diagnosed you with the piles, and he called out their names, beginning with a pile of Schiff-ting-Nadler and ending with K. Hill brushing A.O.C's hair, you just might be a Democrat.

My daddy always said if you are Bernie Sanders and you were told that your pants were unzipped and you replied – uh, it doesn't matter because what can't get up, can't get out.

If your doctor referred you to the local body shop to get that steel toe boot out of your ass, you just might be a Democrat.

If you have to brush your hair for some lice in order to have meat with your rice, you just might be a Democrat.

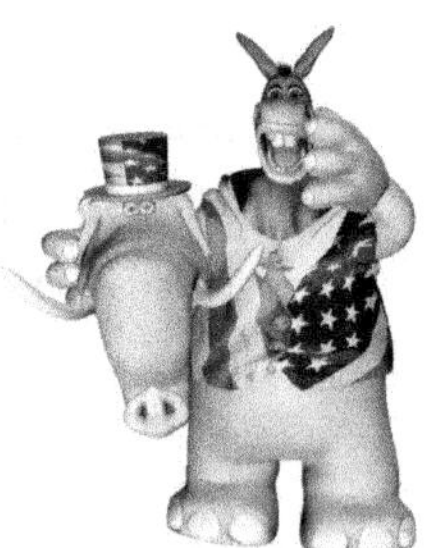

If you are a glittering jewel of total ignorance, you just might be a Democrat.

My daddy always said what were Jeffery Epstein's last words before the 'deep state' pulled the trap door of the gallows? "It was more than I could do to keep from dying, but the ones I knew too much on, didn't want me to remain. Besides, my ass just couldn't take anymore jail house pain."

If you believe the flies flying around Adam's pile of Schiff are Republican flies, you just might be a Democrat.

If every time you have visitors you have to beg to borrow 'the man of the house' pants from your wife, you just might be a Democrat.

If your anus is being used as a docking port for space probes, you just might be a Democrat.

If your answer to the question you were just asked is, "it's not about me," you just might be a Democrat.

If you believe Jane Fonda, Nancy Pelosi and Joy Behar change their own diapers, you just might be a Democrat.

My daddy always said when the Democrats in both Houses were tested, almost all of them tested positive for the Impeachtrumpvirus.

If the content on this page is above your intelligence pay grade, you just might be a Democrat.

If your tally-wacker is drawing disability Social Security, you just might be a Democrat.

If you found the kitty in bed with your dog and your dog is your husband and your maid is your kitty, will you put on that brave face and finally admit, you just might be a Democrat?

If you went Christmas shopping for a left-handed pencil, you just might be a Democrat.

If you use your dandruff to flock your Christmas tree, you just might be a Democrat.

If your yard sale has turned into a tired sale, "tired of waiting on a gov-ment check,' you just might be a Democrat.

If you waited all day to be the last one in line so you could say hello to your cousin Eddie who works at the DMV, you just might be a Democrat.

My daddy always said if you owe over ten-thousand dollars to your local strip club and the I.R.S. but can only afford to pay twenty dollars a month, don't call anyone… there's no help for you.

If your doctor tells you that you don't have a beautifully tanned California bunghole – that you have a donkey dung hole, you just might be a Democrat.

If you have feathers in your teeth from the bird your cat caught because you were fighting over who gets to eat first, you just might be a Democrat.

If the rat in your hand is from the two in your bush, you just might be a Democrat.

My daddy always said 'fracking!' It's what Democrat brains need in order to understand zero plus zero equals zero.

If your condition's condition doesn't know what condition your condition is in, you just might be a Democrat.

My daddy always said President Trump's new song and slogan for 2020 should be, 'I did it all by myself – all by myself. I had no help from the do-nothing Democrats.'

If the pee in your pea soup is from the penis of the pin-head waiter and you left a tip, you just might be a Democrat.

If Santa Claus took you off his naughty or nice list and put you on his never ever again list, you just might be a Democrat.

If your quid wasn't a pro and didn't know how to ho in Ukraine and now you don't have the quo and all you have is trying to pin the tail on another donkey, "duh," you just might be a Democrat.

If your farts would gag a maggot and you still set them free, you just might be a Democrat.

If you are waiting on Santa Claus to bring you some common sense for Christmas, you just might be a Democrat.

If the beef you had for lunch is what your dog will smell for dinner, you just might be a Democrat.

If you are not the Dutch girl "but, there is always a butt somewhere," you have your fingers in all the holes, 'hello Kitty, Kitty,' you just might be a Democrat.

If the pile of Schiff you had for breakfast gave you indigestion, and the mound of Pelosi & Schiff you had for lunch gave you diarrhea, and you turn on the TV to get your fake news for dinner, you just might be a Democrat.

My daddy always said what did the Russian stripper say to the California Congressman on their date? "Word! You need to go dive into the commode and flush it because you smell like a pile of Schiff."

If you've ever sat straddle of a fence and hurt your gonads then blamed the fence, you just might be a Democrat.

If you and your wife can't leave your house at the same time because you share one brain cell between the two of you, you just might be a Democrat.

If your poor old grandma is pole dancing at the local strip club to support you and your wife between gov-ment checks, you just might be a Democrat.

If your daddy was a snowflake and your momma was a snowflake and you need a safe space, you just might be a Democrat.

If you live in L.A. and you're a movie star but you farted in your sleep and the Fire department had to evacuate the entire block and you blamed it on 'ass hole warming,' you just might be a Democrat.

If you think you are owed everything, but you have never worked for anything, you just might be a Democrat.

My daddy always said what did Nancy Pelosi say to the Democrat House Members after the impeachment of President Trump? "Hemorrhoids for sale or rent. A.O.C.'s are only 50 cents, Omar's... only a dime, bag of Schiff, flies included – f-r-e-e.

If the go in your got has turned to a no in your not and the ha in your has was replaced with "did have," you just might be a Democrat.

My daddy always said what did President Trump say when bite-me Biden wanted to take him out behind the barn? "I'm not a Democrat or a goat. So, Joe, you will have to rethink that. You might try poke-a-hontas. I hear she can't get no traction or satisfaction."

If you have ever been to a "mad at a gas car" rally, not the island but the protest, you just might be a Democrat.

If the demons in your skull are full from eating Schiff's crats and you still believe Demon - crats don't lie, you just might be a Democrat.

My daddy always said doctors are showing concern for the spread of the stupid virus. "This virus is spreading like wildfire out of control throughout a large group of people who refuse to 'shelter in place' and 'practice social distancing.' However, their asinine actions finally proves 'stupid is as stupid does.'

If you are a 'bung-hole' but-butt your biggest supporter is your girdle, you just might be a Democrat.

If you were dropped on your head as a baby and you grew up not knowing the difference between "if," "and," or "butt," you just might be a Democrat.

If you gladly gave up your crotch berries to grovel at the feet of Nancy pee loosely, you just might be a Democrat.

If you believe the fake news on TV stations, pee loosely, pencil neck, and no-nads Waddler fed you at breakfast and then you ate it again for lunch, you just might be a Democrat.

My daddy always said how are all the cuckoos going to show off their bung hole suntans at The Emmys? They should just drop their drawers, get on their hands and knees, crawl backwards to the microphone and talk out of their ass. This would make much more sense than what comes out of their mouths.

If the 'hope and change' cost you your job, your car, your house and you still look for the "D" when you vote, you just might be a Democrat.

My daddy always said what did the Democrats say to the Republicans? 'Just hunker down, bend over and we'll let you know when we are through screwing you.'

If you don't know the difference between bull Schiff and talking Schiff, you just might be a Democrat.

If you believe Sheryl Crow only uses two squares of toilet paper to wipe her bony ass in order to save trees, you just might be a Democrat.

If you use your skid marked underwear to wipe the sweat from under your arms before you make love, you just might be a Democrat.

If you are one of the ones that rushed to California to get your bung hole a suntan and you had to stand in line behind Nanny pee loosely and fake-a-hontas Warren, you just might be a Democrat.

If that hairball you just coughed up is from your neighbor's kitty- here kitty, kitty – kitty, here kitty "cough" "hair" "cough" "cough," damn; what a kitty, you just might be a Democrat.

If you are having dreams of fake-a-hontas Warren riding a red horse wearing nothing but a feather in her hair and a tomahawk in her left hand, god you're sick, or you just might be a Democrat.

My daddy always said what did Alexandria Ocasio Cortez ask the gastrologist when she went in for a colonoscopy? "Doctor, while you are in there can you get the Republicans out of my head?"

If you had to smell the farts from hard balls Chris Matthews and Eric Swalwell's impeach Trump farting contest, you just might be a Democrat.

If the bed you shared last night with a ho from the Ho house was discovered to be your wife and she reminded you that you're Chinese and your last name is Ho, you just might be a Democrat.

If you had to eat your partridge in a pear tree for Christmas dinner, you just might be a Democrat.

If the Republican you had for dinner was so good you ordered another one for dessert, you just might be a Democrat.

My daddy always said when A.O.C. caught Nancy Pelosi pissing on the House podium and gavel, she asked, "Nanny, why you pee?" Nancy said, "Honey, when you get to be my age you learn to mark your territory before the beavers and balls attack."

If you call your momma "baby," you just might be a Democrat.

If you stuck your head up Nancy Pelosi's ass to have lunch but – butt, you couldn't tell if it was m-peaches or dried plums, you just might be schiffting from Republican to be a Democrat.

If you are experiencing strange hallucinations and you've been around that crazy Indian, fake – a – hontas, snorting politics, you just might be a Democrat.

If your name is Bernie Sanders and you won't bend over for the squad to kiss your ass, you just might be a Democrat.

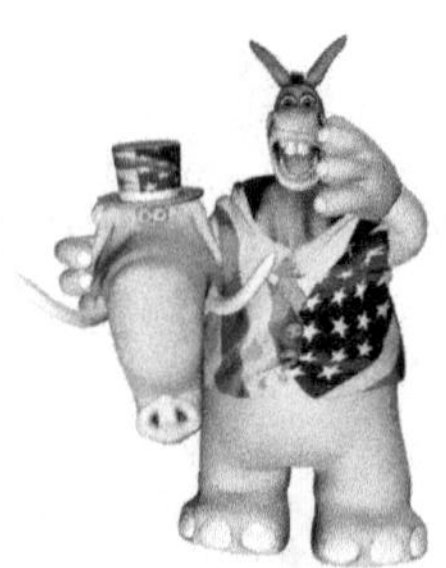

My daddy always said I can fix you up, but you'll need to brush that tooth of yours because you know how Hillary loves those Wall Street deplorables.

If you don't know a thing or two about a thing or two, you just might be a Democrat.

If your job is trying to plug all the holes in Nancy pee loosely's leaks, you just might be a Democrat.

My daddy always said how can the Gov-ment expect people to practice social distancing when half can't even spell it and the other half are so damn happy because now they won't have to smell it, but all they know is that old Birdfinger is right in the middle of everything.

If the genes in your jeans don't know the difference between bare naked and butt naked, you just might be a Democrat.

If you are not Megan Markel but – butt, you have a Harry ass with a Dutch-ass title and your queen mom just repossessed your crown before you left town, you just might be a Democrat.

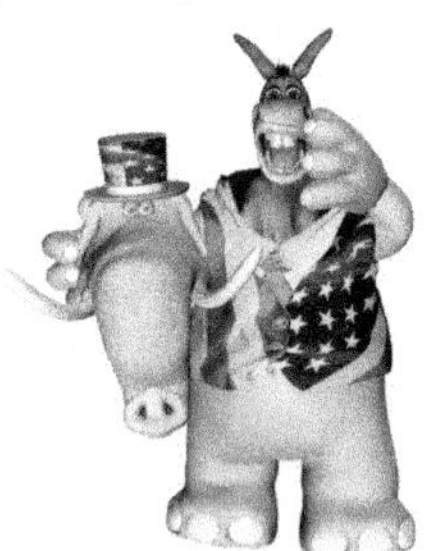

If you own a hot food delivery truck and the customers have tagged it all over with the name, 'Hotturd Express,' you just might be a Democrat.

My daddy always said it's not about the gears in what you drive, it's about what's between the ears when you drive it.

If you are from Florida and your only excitement is getting tased, you just might be a Democrat.

If you thought a peace flag in a pasture full of bulls would stop one of them from loading your ass up with a set of horns, you just might be a snowflake Democrat.

My daddy always said what did Nancy Pelosi and Chuck Schumer say to President Trump and Mitch McConnell about the stimulus package? "Old Mitch is already our snitch so just bend over Mr. President. You're about to get the biggest stimulus in the history of the world and we're not using any Vaseline."

If you married your first cousin and you are not from Mississippi, you just might be a Democrat.

If your doctor said you had a pre-existing condition and he just couldn't fix stupid, you just might be a Democrat.

My daddy always said does someone you know have that dead fish or old goat smell like the members of the U.S. Senate and House of Representatives? There's a cure for that, it's called Polecat Ass Wipes. Vote yours out from: "polecatasswipesforyourstinkingass.com" today.

If your bank lost interest in you, you just might be a Democrat.

If the dream you are chasing is living with poke, rolls, and grits, you just might be a Democrat.

If the beef with your beer taste like pork barrel promises and you keep voting the spider barking windbags back in office, you just might be a Democrat.

If your Congressman daddy takes your Democrat mother on free trips – on the taxpayer's dollars and you think that's okay, you just might be a Democrat.

If you voted for Hillary Clinton and you still don't know why, you just might be a Democrat.

My daddy always said you have heard of Little Caesars but – butt have you heard of 'dirty old geezers?' "Slick Willie" needed someone pulling on his nob – Monica got the job. The "Cos" didn't want the women to feel – so he gave them a little roofie pill. "Weinstein" controlled all the power – so he could take 'it' from any actress, any day, at any hour. "Spacey" 'well' all of you have heard the static. Pity he was born with a lot of space in his attic.

If you are married to a fun gal that has a fungal disease, you just might be a Democrat.

If Santa Claus left you an I.O.U. this Christmas because you haven't paid for last year's Christmas gifts, you just might be a Democrat.

If you broke one of your horns while dancing with the devil, you just might be a Democrat.

If your nose was pulled out of Nancy Pelosi's ass so she could deliver the impeachment papers to the Senate, you just might be a Democrat.

If the kitty in your caboodle was brushed by Katie Hill, you just might be a Democrat.

If you failed the question on what color is the White House, you just might be a Democrat.

My daddy always said when a T.V. reporter said in his, "Here's Hoping" report, that he was hoping to cast a big wide net, one big enough to catch Hillary for reentry into the Presidential race. But – there's always a butt – a talk radio host informed the reporter that they stopped making whale nets years ago. However, there would always be hope in Arkansas. Hope that Hillary would just ride off into the Benghazi sunset.

If the only antique in your house is your ass, you just might be a Democrat.

If you are looking for somebody who has nobody but has more money than anybody, you just might be a Democrat.

If you advertised your ass gas for sale as 'natural gas,' you just might be a Democrat.

If the storage space between your ears is empty, you just might be a Democrat.

If you call your husband and ask him where he's at and he answers I'm in Tooson, and the background noise doesn't convince you he's not in Tucson, Arizona, you just might be a Democrat.

My daddy always said since Nancy Pelosi and Chuck Schumer both talk out of their asses; can they use depends as their Covid19 masks?

If you are one of the two men and a goat love triangle, you just might be a Democrat.

If you wake up needing your booty judged by the booty judge himself, you just might be a Democrat.

My daddy always said what did the mother say to her two daughters as they were walking Nancy Pelosi up the driveway for a social distance dinner? "You girls will have to disinfect that bag before you can bring it in the house."

If your baby daddy bought baby shower gifts for your baby, and his other boo – who-who-whoooo - at the same time, you just might be a Democrat.

If you have a muffin top waist, and a Mount Everest size ass, and you wear panty waist jeans while sitting in judgement of lawbreakers, you just might be a Democrat.

My Daddy always said what did the Democrat leaders send Hillary for Christmas? A Christmas card with a picture of a Peloton inside.

If you support Nanny P. in her effort to sell all the piles of homeless Schiff in San Francisco as Democrat monuments, you just might be a Democrat.

My daddy always said almost heaven... sardines and beans, they always blow a hole in the seat of my jeans. I'm always looking around to see if that fart dropped something on the ground. Here's hoping it's just stink and not round.

If you know that Nancy's witch hunt is a sham and Schiff's pencil neck is from looking for poo, why can't you put the sham and the poo together and wash Nadler's nads and get that Mad Dog 20/20 look off his face? If A.O.C. could pull that off then her three comrades could say, I, we, no you just might be a Democrat.

My daddy always said what was the Democrat Congressman's defense when he was arrested with a hooker? "Your honor, we are under a shelter in place order. That hooker had a place I wanted to shelter in so how can you even think of fining me for a little ten toes up – ten toes down?"

If the highway in your life only has one lane, you just might be a Democrat.

If your doctor told you your rear end needed checking and you drove to Jiffy Lube, you just might be a Democrat.

If you bought one of the turds on eBay that Nancy Pelosi's San Francisco district was trying to sell in order to put a Porta Potty on every corner, you just might be a Democrat.

My daddy always said he could never understand Wynona Ryder. He couldn't understand why she let people ride her when she wasn't even wearing a saddle.

If the one cell in your brain started to corrode and you went to a proctologist for help, you just might be a Democrat.

If at your house you can't tell whether it's rained a little or a lot, you just might be a Democrat.

If you believe fake-a-hontas Warren can be president of anything other than her wigwam, you just might be a Democrat.

If you are Lizzy Warren and old commie Bernie drove the bus that ran over your high cheek bone dreams, "Lizzy," you just might be a Democrat.

If you and your wife play name that prune fart after an oatmeal and prune breakfast, you just might be a Democrat.

My daddy always said what did the gas man say to Nancy Pelosi during a video call? "Nanny pee, from the looks of you, I wouldn't want to smell thee."

If the May in your December is so old, they can't remember if it was May or December when they forgot what they needed to remember, and all you gave them was a string for their finger, you just might be a Democrat.

My daddy always said grandpa found him a new squeeze named Soonass. She kept telling him, soon as you sign a new Will, you will get some Soonass.

If the broom in your closet has been ridden by Nancy Pelosi, you just might be a Democrat.

If your cousin is Eddie and your wife is Betty and you caught her shagging him, they just might be Democrats.

If you lost your grandma's thong in a poker game, you just might be a Democrat.

My daddy always said since everybody is practicing social distancing, could it – would it be possible for some to "unpractice, unsocial, undistance themselves," just to feel another booty? You know, someone's booty other than their own. Maybe this could happen when they run out of toilet paper and have to use their birdfinger as a corn cob replacement.

If you believe L A stands for Los Angeles, Louisiana or lower Alabama and not Lard Ass, you just might be a Democrat.

If your I.Q. is the same as a turnip, you just might be a Democrat.

If your momma took one look at you when you were born then tried to put you back in the oven for a do over, you just might be a Democrat.

If your momma is married to your husband's first wife, you just might be a Democrat.

If the feathers in your teeth came from Jennifer Garner's dead chicken, Colonel George, you just might be a Democrat.

If your parents named you Squirrely but your friends call you Düf-ass, you just might be a Democrat.

My daddy always said somebody should tell Nancy Pelosi that the beaver she wears on her head is out of style and always crooked.

If you swear the tree you hit while avoiding a D.U.I. check point was drunk, you just might be a Democrat.

If you bought one of the lies that network news was selling about President Trump, you just might be a Democrat.

If you identify as one of the flies following Nancy Pelosi around waiting for your in-between-the-cheeks-dinner, you just might be a Democrat.

If smelling your own farts is the only enjoyment you get out of life, you just might be a Democrat.

If you are so stupid you can't even get on the Democrat's impeachment list, you just might be a Democrat.

My daddy always said what did the chi-coms and Democrats say to America about the Corona Virus? "Made in China" by us to buy U.S.

If you are fake-a-hontas Warren and you call the Redman Pest Control to get your beaver bugs sprayed, you just might be a Democrat.

If you burnt all the hair off your ass while roasting your nuts at an open campfire and all your bunghole got was blistered instead of tanned, you just might be a Democrat.

My daddy always said what's the best thing that could happen to the crazed impeach looneys? To be south of the border wall when the last brick is put in place, with no keys to unlock the gate.

If you think the weaker of the House is smarter than the hair that fell off President Trump's ass, yep, you just might be a Democrat.

My daddy always said when House Nanny and shotgun Joe went to the doctor holding hands and sipping Hillary's hope, both wanted to know why their masks were covered with flies. Doctor T said, "Really, I cannot believe all you one brain cellers don't know that the mask goes on your face, not your ass."

If you can't read between the lines, then get yourself a gallon of Hillary's Mad Dog 20/20 wine, that'll get you right in between those lines and by then, you'll either be right or left, or you just might become a Democrat.

If you bought your M.A.G.A. hat at the same Subway shop that you bought your Subway sandwich on a freezing Chicago night, you just might be a Democrat.

My daddy always said silent night, holy night… all the Democrats want to do is fuss and fight. Silent night, holy night… the Democrats can't even get impeachment right. Silent night, holy night… even Rosie O'Donnell knows what the Democrats are doing to President Trump just ain't right.

If the fast track you're on in life is slower than Harvey Weinstein practicing bend over Benny with his walker on the way to prison, you just might be a Democrat.

If you are from pun-job and you don't like poontang, you just might be a Democrat.

My daddy always said if the upper House of Congress is known as the Senate, pray tell what is the lower House of Congress? It's 'Schiff's Porta potty.'

If your "Ain't Bessie" moos and chews her cud and you introduce her as your better half, you just might be a Democrat.

My daddy always said what did Nancy Pelosi say to Adam Schiff? "Adam, I know you have lost your sense of smell, but would you please get your nose out of my tail."

If you are from Arkansas and you marry someone from Illinois and you get your bunghole tanned by someone from California, you just might be a Democrat.

If you use your ear wax for lip balm so you won't stick to Nancy Pelosi's ass and it's your Schiff on the ground, you just might be a Democrat.

If your camel toe was used as a safety deposit box by the Democratic committee of, 'you ain't seen nothing yet,' you just might be a Democrat.

If you think being a movie star makes you smarter than a rock, you just might be a Democrat.

My daddy always said what was Beto O'Rourke's nickname on the campaign trail? "Turd man of old el-pass-a-load."

If the price for your vote has lost its value and now all you get is some south end wind, you just might be a Democrat.

If you don't care if it's a service dog or a check engine light dog, as long as it gets you into the strip club, you just might be a Democrat.

My daddy always said what did the older member of Congress say to the smoking hot new member of Congress? "As you ho – don't forget there are some who like to mow."

If you believe the United States is your sugar daddy and should pay for all your sugar babies, you just might be a Democrat.

My daddy always said when Megan McCain announced she was pregnant only two questions were asked. Who did she have to pay and how much did she have to pay them?

If you are House leaker, Nancy Pelosi, and you have sat through Trump's State of the Union speech and your adult diaper is full of Schiff and you know your stooges have spent all the House budget on trying to find some um' peach seeds, and Sheryl Crow used the last two squares of toilet paper on her bony ass, and all that was left in all the Johns and Janes were empty cardboard sleeves, but you knew walking back to one of the Johns or Janes your diaper would develop your name sake and begin to leak Schiff all down your legs, but there were no trees around for leaves to wipe the dooty – there were no corn cobs for the booty, then like any 'one-brain celler' you saw paper and the idea light went off! "Paper Ass Wipe" – "Ass Wipe Paper," this is a no brainer. I don't have a big ass so if I tear this in half, I can wipe now and have some for later. So, with every tear I'm happy as a Charmin bear. All I need is some ex-lax to help me get rid of that last um' peach seed. Oh, now to pencil in a Trump rally to find out what's up the next peach seed alley and finally admit, I'm just another Democrat dimwit.

My daddy always said half the people driving are crazy as hell, and the other half are going insane trying to stay out of their way.

If you are Joe Biden and you called your only woman supporter a lying dog-faced horse's ass dipstick and she replies, "Pappy Joe, I'm your daughter," – 'Uncle Joe,' you just might be a Democrat.

If you are one of the Californians that elected number 2 for your representative and all he's done is chase his imagery Trump tail while piles of Schiff cover the sidewalks, parks, business doorways, and private property, Birdfinger has one question for you. How is that sanctuary city with streets of Schiff working out? Even a birdbrain thinks, you just might be a Democrat.

If you married someone for better or worse and all you're getting is the worse, you might want to admit they just might be a Democrat.

If you don't know the difference between a corn-hole and the corn hole, don't ask Google or everyone will know, you just might be a Democrat.

If sometimes we rescue dogs and sometimes dogs rescue us, I'm not saying, but Trump did rescue Nancy Pelosi. Could it be she's really just a Chupacabra and not his dog… or could it be, she just might be a Democrat.

My daddy always said Mayor De Blasio, you asked for rats to rat on fellow New Yorkers; well, I am rating. I saw this bubble head bleach blonde bent over the railing of her apartment and her neighbor was "venting – her – lator." He has been venting her everyday since you ordered the shelter in place. For my reward for being a rat, can you order him to vent me, too?

If you have diarrhea more than once a week, be careful, it could run in your genes or, you just might be a Democrat.

If you have enough dust bunnies under your bed to start a rabbit ranch, you just might be a Democrat.

If the pilot in your program could only fly after smoking crack, you just might be a Democrat.

My daddy always said what did Nancy Pelosi say to 'the poor,' 'the homeless,' 'the unemployed,' and 'the hungry' after bragging about the two fifty thousand dollar stainless steel zero degree freezers she bought during the Corona Virus crisis that are packed full with sixty thousand dollars' worth of gourmet ice cream? "Let them eat Schiff."

If you have a hammered toe because your wife caught you playing sugar daddy to her grandma, you just might be a Democrat.

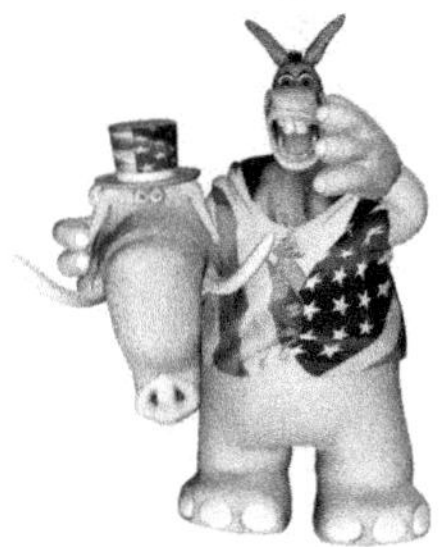

If you believe butt cheeks is one word and you have to spread them apart to see if you are 'to be or not to be,' you just might be a Democrat.

If you are Chris Matthews and Eric Swalwell, what will you forever be known for? Raising your leg and burning the hair off your ass as you broke the sound barrier with a gut-wrenching fart on hard balls new news program called "hard farts?" Some of the staff are still in quarantine down at the mortuary and the rest are in detox at the Betty Ford clinic. Even so, the show must go on… so come one, come all ye' Democrats, crawl up old Chris's leg and be the first to smell the air biscuits. That way everyone can proudly say, you just might be a Democrat.

My daddy always said when fake-a-hontas Warren drops a number duce, is it with or without her fake papoose?

If you have feasted on the buffet of the seven deadliest sins "pride – lust – greed – gluttony – envy – sloth – anger," and your election "erection" for m-peach Trump has lasted longer than four years, you just might be a Democrat.

My daddy always said geez Louise! What the hell did you eat with those peas? You smell like what Nancy Pelosi looks like when she has been in her chambers playing with Schiff.

If you are the person who tried to hire the Nation's largest law firm for your slipped and farted in church lawsuit, you just might be a Democrat.

My daddy always said if you are a wife as Mayor Pete says he is – what in the world do you call your Va-jay-jay? "Anuspainus."

If you look like a lie, walk like a lie, talk like a lie, well, you just might be a Democrat.

If the hair with whiskers you wear on your head was made in China, you just might be a Democrat.

If some people know your name and other people know your game but – butt, everybody knows you're insane, you just might be a Democrat.

If we break up, I'll be fine, but you must know that our dog will be smelling more farts than mine. Katie won't be brushing my hair because I just can't go there. But – 'butt' your phone pics of your pants around your knees just proves, like all socialists, you aim to tease- but – 'butt.' Really, don't be silly, I already suspected, you just might be a Democrat.

My daddy always said what did Michael Jackson sing when he and Lisa Marie Presley were on their honeymoon? Do you think I'm just a Hunk of Burning Love, or nothin' but a Hound Dog?

If you are Jerold Nadler and you have spent so much time with Nancy Pelosi and her squad that you are beginning to smell like fish, you just might be a Democrat.

If you are Chuck-U- or Nanny Pee, just what are you singing to all the Republicans and Trumpsters? "We don't need no education- we don't need no thought control- after all we are just Schiff on Trump's wall. Hey, Republicans, leave our dumb asses alone! After all we're just Democrats against it all and Trump's damn wall. Besides, nobody can fix stupid, not even Trump. Let us simmer with the sorrow of knowing, we just might be Democrats."

My daddy always said when Nanny pee loosely's hairstylist was caught reading fifty ways to style a beaver wig, Nanny pee said, "In my day it was called a cooter and to this day, I think my cooter is drunk as old Cooter Brown because nobody in their right mind wants my cooter around.

If you voted for the one, the only, ohow moomoofuku, you just might be a Democrat.

My daddy always said why did they call Kamala Harris, Kamala-hairless? Because old Willie Brown done wore all the hair off.

If you keep running out of the house screaming geez Louise, why in the hell do you keep eating those peas, you just might be a Democrat.

My daddy always said if you're a Win-dixie dyke, could you love a Liberal lipstick wearing New York Yankee Liberal Democrat as much as you could a Coonass lipstick wearing Conservative Democrat, or would they both have to convert to bootyism?

If Katie Hill had the fire down below but – butt, Nancy Pelosi said not everybody likes a bear-cuda so she sent her little mole hill back to Cal-that-gal-is-horny-forn-I-a before she became a mountain in the swamp. Come on Katie, you cannot let Nancy take away 'your quid' – 'your pro' – 'your quo.' Do like Mrs. Johnson did in 'Harper Valley P.T.A.,' bare that cuda, spill the beans, you know all their secrets, come on, open up- tell the world girl, you just might be a Democrat.

If you and the rest of the world are still wondering what Nancy Pelosi, Speaker of the House, was mumbling after ripping up President Trump's State of the Union Speech… here it is. The riddle was solved and brought to you by none other than the 'hollow head Hollywood lip reading, bunghole tanning, pole dancing society of one brain-cellers' "Is butt cheeks one word or do I need to spread mine apart to see if I just might be a Democrat?"

My daddy always said a copy of Nancy Pelosi's letter to Santa Claus was recently revealed on something that resembled a fake newscast. "Dear Santa, I wrote you in 2018 asking for a peaceful and quiet 2019, but all you put under my tree were porta potties filled with Schiff."

If you have "Found" problems; you found out your wife is smarter than you. You found out your children have spent your retirement and their inheritance but still won't move out of your newly mortgaged house. You found out that the money you lost at the casino belonged to the bank you worked for and then you found out the handcuffs you're wearing are too tight. You found out whether it's rain or piddle - they both splatter, and you found out the bottom line is… it just doesn't matter because, you just might be a Democrat.

If your nickname is fake – a – hontas and you sing, "O – say can you see, lying paid off big time for me. I ripped off the Indians, laughing all the way to the bank, what more do I need to say, except, I just might be a Democrat."

If you think every Democrat has nothing but good intentions, you're either as dumb as a Democrat or, you just might be a Democrat.

If you believe assholes are free because you get one when you're born and you support all the others you elect at the ballot box, you just might be a Democrat.

If Nancy Pelosi is constipated and sitting on the throne saying, "come on out, Schiff… I know you're in there. You gotta get out of that place even though we both know it's the last thing you'll ever do. Give up! Fall out, I need the room, so my bony ass can fit on my broom." You have to agree Nancy is cray-cray or, she just might be a Democrat.

My daddy always said if an elephant's foot covers an acre, what does its tail cover? Schiff's new hoax hole, that's what it covers.

If you were one of the Pilgrims at Plymouth Rock and fake – a – hontas Warren was there to greet you, doing cartwheels with no underwear on, and you ran to board the next flight to Hawaii so you could watch Tulsi Gabbard do her hula dance, you just might be a Democrat.

If Nancy Pelosi sings 'let it pee, let it pee,' every time she sits on the potty and you think that's normal, you just might be a Democrat.

If you believe Mitt Romney is just a typical Democrat while the rest of the world knows he's a pompous ass, you just might be a Democrat.

My daddy always said since the Democrats added Ex-lax to their quantitative easing arsenal of arsess, the log jams will soon be broken and all their common sense will be flushed down the toilet without a single square of toilet paper to wipe away all the Schiff M-peach seeds.

If you are Jeffery Epstein and you finally make it to the end of that long dark tunnel and Satan says, 'you're late, no soup for you!" You're either having the nightmare from hell or, you just might be a Democrat.

If you painted your lips, rolled and curled your dyed hair, just to take your fake Indian ass to the Democrat's nightmare on the dim-wit de-bait stage, oh, Liz… keep your feckless – A – in your wigwam, play with your papoose before Tulsi cooks your goose exposing the fact that, you just might be a Democrat.

If you are a millennial and you called 911 because you saw a light on your car's dash that said door ajar, and you couldn't unscrew the top, you just might be a Democrat.

If you are a Democrat, how many 'damn, I'm sorry,' does it take to cover up the Schiff that you piled up over the years? Little Mikey Bloom boom has said he is sorry, so get over it! What's a little frisk and feel among those who can say Mike, you just might be a Democrat?

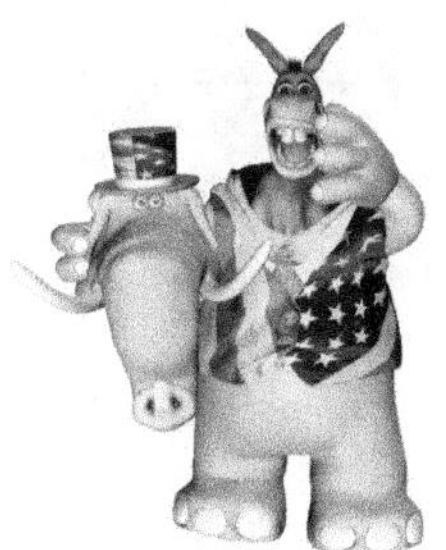

My daddy always said what did the Chinese say about Winston being the first dog in America testing positive for the Corona Virus? "Winston taste good, just like a Corona Virus dog should."

My daddy always said when you are trying to bond with a Democrat, make sure you have enough money to pay their bail.

My daddy always said there is a way to survive the bung hole suntan craze without getting blisters all over your bung hole. Take a clue from Nancy Reagan… Just Say NO!

If you are worried about a slip and fart – it's free unless you get caught. Then it's point the finger or Birdfinger and laugh at the fact, you just might be a Democrat.

If you are a Democrat lesbian, can you cross the isle for some lipstick loving from a Republican or do you have to shop with the you just might be a Democrat gene pool?

My daddy always said thunder doesn't always happen when it's raining, and farts don't always happen when your straining.

If the whiskey in your glass taste like the smell of Nancy's ass, you might be standing too close or, you just might be a Democrat.

If you are the "advice" that R.G.B. gave to A.O.C., who couldn't understand and passed it on to Jay Z - the sit down man for the National Anthem- that this is the only country on the planet that gives freely to everyone, including all the... you just might be Democrats.

If you are Adam Schiff and your hatred is so ingrained in your envious brain that you don't have sense enough to get out of the dumbass donkeycrat rain – also, your neck and nose keep getting longer, "word" Jared Kushner could at least run the country; and the world knows you can't even run a little old fake impeachment… so comrade Schiff, you win the prize of, you just might be a Democrat.

If the Democrats just tweeted out 'when you need money and you need it fast, just pucker up and kiss our ass,' and you still vote for them, well sir-sis or sis-sir, you just might be a Democrat.

My daddy always said if you reach out for the K.Y. jelly on the nightstand but – butt, instead you grab a tube of Bengay, after that scream, what do you sing? "Burn, baby burn, my bung hole is burning!"

My daddy always said hear-ye, hear-ye, hear-ye. To all ye Democrats, Liberals, Socialists and flat earth believers; please do your part and practice social distancing before you fart.

If your other half changed her name to Small Business and put a flashing neon sign in the front yard advertising 'a little Small Business for sale,' and you were operating the cash register when the po-po arrived, you just might be a Democrat.

My daddy always said if you think becoming a politician is quick and easy, not slick and greasy, you just might be a Democrat.

If you are Brad Pitt, you don't need forty-five seconds to prove you are an idiot. Fifty percent of Americans have known for years that you are a one brain cell stooge. The rest are just now discovering your real problem, you just might be a Democrat.

My daddy always said you should never try to pet grandma's kitty when she is at the Democratic National Convention.

If you are a local hooker and you named your ass Honey – then you begin advertising in the local paper, 'Local Honey for Sale,' you just might be a Democrat.

My daddy always said when Kim Kardashian offered to block the southern U.S. border with her ass, Kanye spoke up and said, "But, "butt" that would leave no way for "José."

If you see a shadow on the ground from the sky by a fly over bird and you feel something wet and gooey hit the top of your head it's only Birdfinger letting you know, you just might be a Democrat.

My daddy always said social distancing is the greatest 'invention' since the invention of the silent but deadly fart. Now if they could just socially distance all the elected Democrats except Katie Hill and Tulsi Gabbard. If they sent half of the Democrats to the North Pole and the other half to the South Pole, imagine all the hair that could get brushed.

My daddy always said during a pandemic the only two things in life that make it worth living is faster drive thru lanes and no restroom lines.

If you are not intelligent enough to be a Republican, you just might be a Democrat.

My daddy always said if you smell gas and you can't leave the area immediately, you just might be in an elevator with a Democrat.

My daddy always said think about all that you are saying but never say all that you are thinking.

Backward

Once upon a rhyme, there was a time when the rats and cans worked together for the good of the country and its citizens. That was before the two B's – that was before the two C's – that was before the two O's. It was before greed planted the seeds of corruption. It was before what's mine in mine, what's yours is mine.

We are the rats of both Houses of Congress. We are the rats of all the fake news, T.V., print and social media. We are the rats running wild and free. We are the rats that have quarantined all the cats.

When you hear the demon-rats calling, here kitty, here kitty, here kitty, kitty, kitty; come on over to my house so I can play with you kitty. Those rats are not looking for love in all the wrong places. They are looking for stray cats that they can cover with eights and aces, so be careful crossing the road. Chicken Little is not driving the bus.

Birdfinger's Tree Notes

Two B's = Two terms of "W" – we don't know what we don't know – but the war is over.

Two C's = Two terms of Slick Willie – I'm a virgin… I've never had sex with anyone including that woman – Monica Lewinsky.

Two O's = Who Me! Ugh -ugh – ugh – ugh – I didn't do anything, it's the Republicans fault.

The End

Forward

With No Reverse

Butt Something Free for The End

"Mean" while an update on the richest Democrat in Congress a.k.a. Nancy Pelosi, and her position of having sex after 80 while eating gourmet ice cream that cost over $200.00 a pint that is stored in her $100,000.00 dollar twin side by side stainless steel freezers. When the speaker was asked about New York Governor Andrew Crymo and his brother Fredo Crymo complaining about everything from him-roids to her-roids and always wanting more. Nanny said, "That's the reason they can't come to my house. Those two will eat all my ice cream and cry for mo." What about Chuck-u-Schumer? "Well, old Chuckie said he was a small business owner and for once, he was telling the truth. I saw it when his fly was open once and believe me, that was small business." Nanny P. what about that rumor that Johnathon Carl looks like he was breastfed by you Nanny P. every time you were in a porta-potty giving birth to a turd? "What can I say? Some people are just down and dirty." Speaker, is there anything else you would like to address or anyone you would like to undress? "Yes, that rumor that Moses started that I'm the reason God made hemorrhoids may not be true. And last but not least before I end this – if you lick grandma's fingers after she has picked her nose, you just might be a Democrat."

"Now for The Free"

The best review wins a free all-expense paid trip to your anus. You can take one guest with you, but-butt they have to pay for their own Vaseline. There is no reward for ten toes up and ten toes down. There is no reward for ten toes forward or ten toes digging in the ground. But-butt there could be a reward for anyone who knows what color bear grease does Nanny pee "purr-fur," black, brown or Polar?

Reviews Are Free to Post

Butt please don't use baby butt's butt paste on your Beto Texas toast when you post.

Least Now

Get your finger out of it. I wouldn't give you any of it no matter what you do. It ain't that stuff I'm talking about. It's birthday cake I'm talking about so get your finger out of it, before it's the last thing you ever do.

"If"

If you have future plans to visit the peoples house in D.C. watch where you step. There are puddles of pee and piles of Schiff everywhere. Rubber boots cover up the feet but-butt-butt-butt there is nothing that can cover up the smell, until election day.

Another Hilarious Book
by C. Birdfinger

Visit:

www.mydaddyalwayssaid.com

www.ingramcontent.com/pod-product-compliance
Lightning Source LLC
Chambersburg PA
CBHW051500050726
47593CB00005B/2152
* 9 7 8 1 7 3 3 1 4 5 2 9 9 *